Geography

Burma is a land of geographical extremes, featuring great rivers, snow-capped mountains, tropical jungle, and sea. It is mostly a tropical, mountainous country — three-quarters of it lies between the Equator and Tropic of Cancer.

Burma has borders with China, Laos and Thailand to the east, and with India and Bangladesh to the west. The west coast, which forms part of the Bay of Bengal, is separated from the central Burmese Plain by a ridge of mountains known as the Arakan Yoma. These mountains continue running north and effectively divide western Burma from India and Bangladesh. The land mountains are highest in the north but the most southerly peaks rise out of the Indian Ocean to form the Andaman and Nicobar Islands. The west coast of Burma, known as Arakan, is rocky and has many offshore islands.

The south-east of the country, an area known as Tenasserim, is also divided from its neighbour Thailand by a range of mountains. Tenasserim is also known as 'the Burmese panhandle' because of its shape on the map. The coast of Tenasserim is very similar to that of Arakan, with sandy beaches, rocks, and muddy tidal estuaries.

In the extreme north the mountains are extremely rugged and often rise to over 6,000 metres, As a result they have a permanent snow cover.

The great central plain of Burma has two main rivers, the Irrawaddy, and the Sittang. These are divided by yet another mountain range called the Pegu Yoma.

The entire eastern part of Burma is made up of the Shan Plateau which has an average height of about 1,000 metres above sea level.

The lush centre of Burma, site of Pagan.

Rivers, plains and mountains — a natural place to settle.

The Rivers of Burma As in the other countries of Asia the rivers of Burma play a very important part in the life of the nation.

The greatest river is the Irrawaddy. It rises in the mountains of the northern part of the country and flows south through a wide fertile valley which it has helped to create by depositing silt each year during the annual floods. The Irrawaddy is a source of fertile soils and irrigation water, and is also used for transport. It is used by boats for a distance of about 1,500 kilometres inland. At its mouth it has formed a huge fertile delta which grows year by year seawards into the Gulf of Martaban.

A major tributary of the Irrawaddy is the Chindwin which like the Irrawaddy rises in the north and is used for transporting goods.

Further to the east lie the Sittang and Salween Rivers. In earlier times the Sittang was as big as the Irrawaddy, but now a number of streams which once fed the waters of the Sittang flow west into the Irrawaddy. Although the Sittang can only be used by boats for a short distance, it is still important for the floating of logs from the logging areas in the hills to the sawmills further south. The Salween rises in Tibet and flows across the Shan Plateau into which it has cut steep sided gorges and valleys. It is also used for the transport of timber.

All four rivers can flood during the rainy season. In many parts of Burma houses are built on stilts for this reason.

Climate

Burma has a tropical climate with an annual monsoon which comes from the south-west off the Indian Ocean. There are three main seasons. The wet season lasts for about six months from May to October. This is followed by the cool season from November to February. From February to the end of April the temperature and the humidity rise as the hot season prevails until the onset of the rains again. Conditions in the lowlands during this hot season can be uncomfortable and many people seek relief from the heat by going into the mountains.

Although there are three main seasons, the climate varies throughout Burma. The coastal and mountain regions receive the highest rainfall of up to 5080 mm per year. Northern Burma is the driest area, with the annual rainfall averaging about 510 – 1015 mm. Centered around Mandalay is a dry zone which, in some years, can receive less than 500 mm of rainfall. This is because the monsoon loses much of its moisture on the coastal mountain ranges which creates a 'rain shadow' further inland.

Temperatures are affected by altitude. Many of the hill regions are pleasantly cool in the summer, while in the far north the mountain winters can be bitterly cold.

Stilts offer some protection against flooding.

The Environment

Plants

A large part of Burma is covered in tropical forest in which grow the valuable hardwoods such as teak and pyinkado. Elsewhere the type of vegetation to be found varies, dependent upon the rainfall and the temperature. In many coastal areas there are thick mangrove forests, common elsewhere in Asia. Frost does occur in the hill regions above about 800 metres and this means that there is a more open vegetation made up of evergreen oaks, pines, and areas of grassland, scrubby bushes and bracken ferns. The dry area in the centre of Burma also has more open country. Inland along the river courses there are thick growths of reeds and grasses which often reach heights of five metres or more.

Vegetation grows thickly in tropical areas.

Animals

The native animals of Burma are found throughout South-East Asia. Elephants and buffalo are among the most numerous as both are used for work in the teak forests and in the rice fields. In the forests there are many pigs and deer, and in some areas tigers still pose a threat to livestock and occasionally humans. Smaller animals include squirrels and monkeys. Wild cattle can be found in the more open country.

There is a wide variety of bird life, from the birds of prey such as eagles and hawks to the mynahs and crows which live around the towns and villages.

Natives of Burma: the crab-eating macaque and the myna bird.

Numerous reptiles can be found throughout the country as well as a great variety of insect life. Insects range from colourful butterflies to the termites which have destroyed much of the finely carved woodwork to be found on buildings such as temples.

Natural Resources

Power

Burma has large deposits of oil and gas and these have been important in its economy for many years. Oil and petroleum products are exported. One of the most important of these products is wax which is used in the manufacture of explosives, matches, and waterproofing compounds. Oil exploration and production, as well as its sale, is wholly controlled by the Government. There are a number of refineries, for instance at Syriam near Rangoon, and at Chauk further up the Irrawaddy.

Coal deposits are small and the coal is of poor quality. However this is more than made up for by the abundant water resources of the country which can be used for the production of hydro-electricity. About a quarter of the electricity produced in Burma comes from hydro-electric plants.

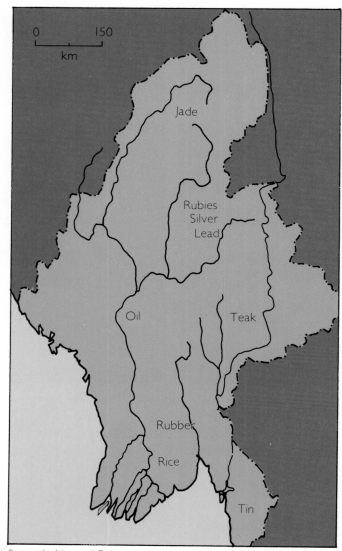

Burma's Natural Resources:

Minerals

The main minerals produced are silver, zinc, and lead. Most of the silver and lead is found in the Shan Plateau area. Tin and tungsten are both mined in Tenasserim and this mirrors Thailand's tin-mining activities on the same peninsula.

Gold is found in small quantities and most of this is produced from river deposits on a part-time basis by local people.

Limestone is widely quarried both for the cement industry and for buildings. Jade, which is used for jewellery and other ornaments, is also quarried. In the past this was exported mainly to China. Marble, a form of limestone, is another rock of commercial importance.

Jade and gold Buddhas sit 100 metres deep in the limestone Pindaya Caves. Shan.

Precious stones such as rubies and sapphires are found in a number of river- deposited soils. Among the more unusual materials that are mined is amber which is a fossilised form of tree resin.

Burma's History

Like all the other States in this region, Burma has a long and complicated history. Its borders have changed many times over the centuries as different tribes and kingdoms have fought for possession of land.

The first recorded people of Burma were known as the Pyu, but where they came from is unclear. They had a number of different capitals and were most powerful in the north. But in the eighth century A.D. the kingdom of Pyu was overrun by Thai people who had been driven out of the Province of Yunnan in China by the Chinese.

At about the same time in the south of the country the Mon people established themselves and had their capital between the deltas of the Salween and Sittang Rivers at Thaton. Both the Indians and the Arabs were in contact with the Mons and greatly influenced their way of life. Slightly earlier, in the fifth century A.D., Buddhist missionaries from India introduced Buddhism to the southern areas.

The Burmese began to enter Burma at the end of the ninth century A.D. from Tibet. They had probably already come into contact with Buddhism, but they still retained many of their original religious customs.

A bullock-cart rumbles past Pagan monuments.

Burma then was made up of a number of smaller Burmese kingdoms, but in 1044 a King Anawratha took the throne and made his capital at Pagan. Through a series of conquests he made Burma west of the Shan Plateau into a single nation. It is with the reign of Anawratha that the traceable history of Burma begins, because he gave the Burmese their first script which allowed them to write down their stories and chronicles. Anawratha also built many fine pagodas at Pagan and the remains of this once great city can be seen to this day. After his conquest of the Mons in the south, Anawratha ordered all the Buddhist scriptures belonging to them, as well as the monks themselves, to be taken to Pagan. This had an important effect on the development of Buddhism among the Burmese. Until then it had not been practised in its pure form.

The dazzling Shive Dagon Pagoda, Rangoon.

The successors of Anawratha carried on his works, but none of them were as strong in their leadership of Burma as one nation. The end for Pagan began when the Thais were again pushed out of Yunnan by the Tartar tribes under Kublai Khan in the 1200s. The Thais, already established in lands to the east (later to become Thailand), began to push into Burma. At about the same time the Tartar tribes invaded the northern areas of Burma when the Burmese refused to accept Kublai Khan as their overlord. In the south the Mon people with the help of tribes from the Shan Plateau rose against the Burmese rule and regained control of their lands in the south. As a result of all these combined pressures the city of Pagan fell and central and northern Burma remained under the control of the Shans and the Thais for many years.

Centuries of warfare followed between the various tribes and kingdoms in the region.

It was in the seaports of southern Burma which were then controlled by the Mon people that the first contacts with Europeans were made.

The fairytale splendour of the Pagan empire still dominates the landscape.

European Influence   Marco Polo, the Venetian explorer, may have left the first European account of Burma. At the time of the Tartar invasions of northern Burma he was serving in the court of Kublai Khan, the Tartar Emperor of China. The first Europeans to trade with Burma were the Portuguese. This trade was often forced on to the various peoples of the area at the point of a gun. A number of Portuguese merchant adventurers carved out mini-kingdoms for themselves in various parts of South-East Asia at this time.

Following the Portuguese were the Dutch, British and French. But for many years the Burmese refused to deal with the foreigners, or imposed strict rules and high taxes on them. Among the products which the Burmese refused to export was teak. To overcome this both the British and the French built shipyards at Syriam and then sailed the timber away in the form of finished ships.

The British were particularly concerned about the Burmese plans to invade parts of northern India and, in 1824, they landed a force at Rangoon which surrendered immediately. This was the beginning of a series of Burmese – British wars which ended in 1885 when King Thibaw handed over his capital at Mandalay.

Throughout the period of British Rule in Burma there was always a strong independence movement. Independence itself came as a result of the Second World War. When the Japanese forces invaded Burma in 1941 they already had the help of a number of Burmese and by 1942 the British had been driven out of Burma along with the Indian Army, and the Chinese. During the Second World War Japan used British and allied prisoners-of-war to build the infamous Burmese Railway, which cost thousands of lives. The Japanese set up an 'independent' Burmese government, but in reality this was controlled by the Japanese. Eventually a resistance movement grew up against the Japanese who surrendered in 1946 and Britain regained temporary control of Burma.

The boat-palace outside Rangoon is a modern, concrete, floating restaurant.

Independence

In 1947 Britain agreed to full independence for Burma. On 4 January 1948 Burma became an independent republic and, because of the hostility to the British, they also decided to stay out of the Commonwealth.

Constitution and Government

The original Constitution of Burma as an independent republic was based on those of the United Kingdom, the USA, France, and Yugoslavia. It was democratic, that is, it granted all adults the right to vote for their government.

Since Independence, however, there have been many periods of rebellion and unrest. Many of the smaller tribal groups have felt that their interests were being threatened and have turned to violence in an attempt to gain independence from the Government in Rangoon. As a result the military took over the running of the country in 1962. Martial law lasted until 1974 when a new constitution came into being and elections were held, but with only one party to vote for.

Government is by the People's Assembly under the leadership of the State Council which has twenty-seven members. The Head of State is elected by the People's Assembly.

Modern Rangoon. downtown.

Agriculture

Burma has always been an agricultural country. Some seventy percent of the workforce works on the land, and over eighty per cent of the population lives in the countryside.

Most of the agricultural land is situated in the delta areas and along the major river valleys such as the Irrawaddy, the Sittang, and the Chindwin. Irrigation is necessary in some parts, particularly in the central areas. About one million hectares of land are irrigated.

Rice

Throughout Asia rice is the most important crop and Burma is one of the world's leading producers of rice. Today about 14,000,000 tonnes of rice are produced annually and most of this comes from the delta regions, and from the far north where the rainfall is high. Many varieties of rice are grown and some are sun-dried before being offered for sale. There are also numerous by-products of rice. Rice Brokens, which are broken, damaged, or undersize grains have a ready market for starch manufacture and in the brewing industry. Rice bran can be used for animal feed. Oil is also extracted from the bran using chemicals. The oil-extracted bran is also used for feedstuffs and contains a higher proportion of protein than ordinary bran.

Other important grain crops include maize and millet. Pulses, that is beans, are widely grown in a great many varieties. They include butter beans, many types of peas, and lentils.

Planting the next rice-crop.

Cash crops

Cash crops include sugarcane and tobacco. Rubber is grown mainly in the southern panhandle where the temperatures are higher and there is a short dry season. Plants grown especially for the production of vegetable oils are groundnuts and sesame.

Cotton is grown as both a winter crop and a summer crop and supplies much of Burma's own textile industry. The other fibre crop is jute which was grown commercially for the first time in the early 1950s. Jute is sown before the onset of the monsoon and is harvested in August. It is used in the manufacture of gunny bags with the better quality types being sent to carpet manufacture.

Stock Sale: a strong animal is an essential investment.

Livestock

The most important farm livestock are cattle and buffalo. Both are bred as draught animals. Cattle are used in the drier areas, while buffalo are used in the wet and marshy delta regions. Elephants are also widely used in the forests for hauling logs although these are gradually being replaced by heavy machinery.

Food animals include pigs, chickens and goats.

Water buffalo drag teak logs from the Irrawaddy River.

Forestry

The logging industry is Government-controlled. There is a well organised re-planting programme for all forest areas which are harvested for timber. The wasteful extraction methods of the past have now largely disappeared.

Burma is famous for its teak and supplies most of the world demand for this hard and strong wood. It is particularly valuable in shipbuilding as it has unusual water-resisting qualities. The tree itself can grow to heights in excess of 45 metres and may be as much as seven or eight metres around the trunk.

The forests of Burma produce many other varieties of woods. Some are suitable for building, and railway sleepers. Others are better used for turning small objects, and making piano keys and toys.

Apart from timber there are various other forest products. Among these are orchids of which there are many varieties. Gums and resins are used for the manufacture of polishes; turpentine is used in the paint industry and for medicines. There are a great number of plants which have great medicinal value for a variety of complaints. Bamboo is also of some importance. It is used for building, in paper-making, and for products such as fishing rods and light flag poles.

Fisheries

The State owns over seventy fishing vessels, including thirty-two trawlers. Fishing is an important coastal activity and the main fishing fleet is made up of small boats each operated by perhaps two men. Nets can also be controlled from the shore. Fishing also takes place in the rivers and the marshes. In some inland areas, such as around Lake Inle, fishing is a major occupation.

Fishing on Inle Lake — note the leg paddle.

Industry

Industry in Burma today is developing with the help of foreign aid. Until recently manufacturing was in the hands of the village craftsman who produced mainly traditional goods from local materials.

Crafts

Burma is probably most famous for the quality of its silks and woodwork, particularly woodcarving. Many types of wood are used for carving, but teak is the most common. Teak, however, cannot be carved in very fine detail and so designs tend to be bold with large figures. Lacquer is a decorative and protective surface applied to wood, particularly on small items of furniture such as boxes, tables, and screens.

Metalworkers also produce a wide range of goods. These may be of beaten silver or copper, and include items of tableware such as bowls and cutlery as well as fine jewellery. Cast objects make extensive use of bronze and among the largest of these items are bells. Craftsmen in steel still produce a range of knives and swords which are all known as *dahs*.

Intricate designs decorate lacquered baskets and screens.

Embroidered cloth and semi-precious gems mark the end of the Buddhist Lent.

Handwoven cloth, including silks and cottons, are in demand in the markets and are a favourite item with tourists to Burma. Mat and basket makers use a variety of materials for their products including rushes and split bamboo.

Gems   Precious and semi-precious stones are still mined in parts of Burma and rubies, sapphires, jade, and pearls are all used to produce beautiful jewellery.

Among the many craft industries which produce larger everyday items still in use are the bullock-cart and boat-building industries. Both these use the resources of the forest.

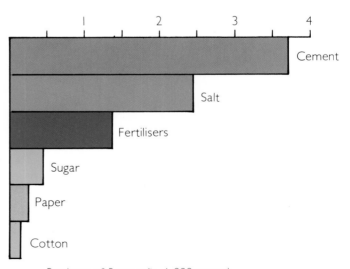

Products of Burma (in 1,000 tonnes)

Factories and Heavy Industry

Most industries until recently were associated with processing agricultural produce. These included rice mills, saw mills and textile factories. The only other major industrial activity was the refining of crude oil which began before World War Two.

Now Burma has more diversity of industry, but it is still not enough to satisfy her own needs, nor to create a large export market for Burmese manufactured goods. Many of the new industries have been set up with assistance from other countries. The processing of farm produce is still an important part of industrial life with a number of sugar mills, cotton spinning and weaving factories, and jute mills. Associated with agriculture are a number of fertiliser factories. Other chemical plants produce medical supplies.

There are a number of cement factories and steel mills, as well as plants which produce building bricks and tiles. Glass is also an important product of Burmese industry, as are salt and paper.

Transport and Communications

Road

Burma has approximately 22,000 kilometres of roads and there is a variety of transport to choose from. For long distance travel buses are available, but these are usually crowded and a number of them are very old, having been converted from trucks which are sometimes over forty years old. In the cities public transport includes taxis which may be saloon cars, utilities, or even three-wheeled vehicles. Trishaws are also used in all but the narrowest streets and although most of these still use 'pedal-power' many of them are now motorised. In most country areas ponycarts are used for passenger transport.

Rail

Rangoon, the capital, is the centre of the rail network which extends to all parts of the country. Some of the long distance trains have sleeper accommodation and a restaurant car. On most stations sellers provide fresh fruit as well as cooked foods such as curries.

Shipping

The inland waterways of Burma have always been of great importance for the transport of goods, particularly timber from the logging camps. Today there are a number of large craft which run trips for tourists. The Inland Water Transport Board controls most of the river traffic, including that on the canals and in the delta areas. Overseas shipping is organised by the Government through its agency known as the Burma Five Star Corporation.

Air

Travel by air in Burma may be by small jet aircraft, or more usually by twin engine propellor driven planes such as the De Havilland Twin Otter, or the Dutch Fokker Friendship. The Burma Airways Corporation flies to five overseas destinations.

Religion and Festivals

Most Burmese are of the Buddhist faith. Buddhism does not have a supreme god and Buddhists do not offer prayers. Although the monks are always looked upon with the greatest respect they are not ministers of religion. The Buddhists use a calendar based on the lunar cycle and so their festivals occur on different dates each year. Each Pagoda, or Buddhist Temple that is in use, has its own celebration every year. There are also national celebrations which commemorate Independence, and a number of national heroes. These are fixed according to the Western calendar and so occur on the same date each year.

Independence Day

Independence Day is celebrated each year on 4 January with plays, dancing, and sports events. Union Day in February commemorates Bogyoke Aung San who united the Burmese people against both the Japanese and the British.

In February, or March, the Buddhist festival of the Full Moon of Taubang marks the start of the rice harvest and offerings are made at the many shrines to Buddha. The Water Festival, or Thingyan, takes place in April. During this the images of Buddha are washed in scented water and this is followed by a water fight and general merry-making. It marks the start of the Buddhist New Year. Buddha's birth is remembered in April/May.

In June/July many young men enter monasteries for a short period. This is the beginning of Waso, which is similar to the Christian Lent. Waso lasts for three months and during this time marriages are forbidden as are most other forms of celebration. In October the festival of Thadingyut marks the end of Waso with a festival of lights. There is much singing and dancing. This is followed in November by another light festival. Christmas Day is a public holiday in Burma.

Thingyou, the Water Festival, marks the Buddhist New Year.

Education

Education is free at all levels from kindergarten up to senior secondary level after which fees must be paid. All children are educated in Burmese, but English is a compulsory second language even in kindergarten. All children receive instruction in reading, writing and maths, as well as in the sciences and a variety of crafts.

Higher education is provided by vocational institutes where students learn trades such as building and vehicle maintenance. The universities provide a wide range of courses and there are special colleges for agriculture, medicine and engineering among others. Some students study through correspondence courses which are organised by the various colleges and universities.

Health and Welfare

Primary health care is provided by rural health centres each of which may serve a number of villages. These centres are staffed by trained people such as midwives, vaccinators, and health visitors. Health assistants receive a two year training which allows them to deal with minor ailments. Serious cases are sent to hospital for treatment by fully trained doctors. One of the most important tasks of the health visitor is to provide advice to villages about the improvement of conditions to prevent the spread of disease.

Health for sale! A homeopath plys his skills.

The Arts

Burmese painting has been influenced by the Chinese, but more by the Indians. In times past painting was part of architecture and was used to decorate the walls and the woodwork of palaces and temples. Most of the subjects were traditional folk tales, or stories from the Buddhist teachings.

As in other countries of South-East Asia, the early writings were mainly in verse form. There was also a separate language used in the official court circles which was much more formal than everyday Burmese. Many works were written in this official Burmese and until the beginning of this century this prevented literature from becoming popular. Eventually books and plays began to be written in the everyday language of the ordinary Burmese people.

Pastel colours and delicate stonework mark the unusual Ahlain Aga Sint Pagoda in Rangoon.

*Yow Pwe (puppet opera)
is very popular.*

The Popular Pwe

Pwe is Burmese drama and it takes three main forms. The *Zat Pwe* is similar to opera, but the music is secondary to the action, unlike western opera where the music is the most important thing. The stories enacted in the *Zat Pwe* are basically traditional, but the players use many modern tricks. They may even include references to the Government, and there are always plenty of jokes and much clowning around.

The *Yoh Pwe* is similar to the *Zat Pwe*, but instead of live performers, puppets are used. At times the puppet *Pwe* is more popular than the live performance.

Song and dance is the main element in the *Yein Pwe*. Again unlike western forms, Burmese dance makes little use of the legs. The action is mainly that of the upper body from the head down to the fingertips.

Music at all these performances is provided by orchestras. Burmese musical instruments include bells, drums, cymbals, gongs, flutes, xylophones, and a type of reed instrument similar to the oboe. The harp is often used in smaller performances.

*Yow Pwe — a horse
gallops across the stage.*

Floating markets are an everyday event.

Food

Rice is, of course, the main food of Burma and is usually eaten with a mild curry. Curries can be made with fish, mutton, pork, chicken, or sometimes beef. A favourite curry sauce for fish is made with oil, garlic, chilli peppers, tomatoes, onions, and small amounts of other spices. It is usual to serve a thin soup called *hinjo* with curry dishes. The Burmese are fond of small side dishes which may contain a very hot spicey fish paste called *ngapigyaw*, or it may be a milder version which is often sweetened with prawns.

Sometimes meat is cooked with potatoes, but the most common method of cooking pork is to fry it with green vegetables added to the hot oil.

Fresh fruit is plentiful all year round in Burma and may be eaten fresh, or as part of a sweet dish such as shredded ice. Pastries and other forms of sweets are popular at all times of the day. Tea is the favourite drink of most Burmese.

Both Indian and Chinese foods can be eaten in Burma and these can be bought at restaurants, or from stalls in the markets and bazaars.

Sport and Recreation

Burma's most popular sport is football (soccer) and the main stadium in Rangoon is named in honour of Bogyoke Aung San. Cricket and hockey both have a small following.

Burmese boxing is similar to Thai boxing in that kicking and barging the opponent are allowed as well as punching.

Chinlon

One of the most popular Burmese sports is Chinlon. In this sport, a small ball made of cane is kept in the air for as long as possible by players who stand in a circle. Any part of the body may be used except the hands. Chinlon requires a great deal of skill to be played properly.

Golf and tennis also attract a number of people.

Canoe racing

One of the most curious sports is canoe racing on the Inle Lake. Instead of sitting down and paddling the craft using their arms to control the paddles, the crew stand up and use their legs to sweep the paddles backwards. In this way canoes can reach high speeds.

In non-sport areas, Rangoon offers a television station, over 400 cinemas throughout throughout the country, theatre, the museum, the zoo. There are also pleasure trips available on the rivers and canals.

'Chinlon' uses a bamboo ball.

Gazetteer

Official name: The Socialist Republic of the Union of Burma (Pyidaungsu Socialist Thammada Myanma Naingngandaw)

Constitution: Socialist Republic

Head of State: The President (U San Yu, elected 1981)

Head of Government: U San Yu. The Prime Minister is U Maung Maung Kha.

Official language: Burmese, but the use of English is allowed

Capital city: Rangoon

Area: 678,000 square kilometres

Population: 36,000,000

Longest River: Irrawaddy River

Climate: The climate varies from north to south. In the south there is a tropical monsoon climate. Temperatures and rainfall are lower in the north. Temperature for Rangoon: Jan. 25°C, July 27°C. Rainfall: 2,616 mm.

Weights and measures: Though the imperial system is used for measurement of distance, both the imperial and metric systems are widely used for all purposes

Currency: The currency unit is the *kyat* which is divided into 100 *pyas*

Religion: At one time Buddhism was the state religion. Now all people are free to practise their own religion.

Airports and shipping: Rangoon has the only international airport. Burma Airways Corporation operates on both domestic and international routes. Ships are an important means of transport using the rivers and canals of Burma.

Agricultural production: The main crops are rice, sugarcane, groundnuts and cotton

Main exports: Agricultural and forestry products, wax, and some minerals

Main imports: Industrial machinery (No reliable figures are available)

Main trading partners: All foreign trade is handled by the government (No figures available)

Treaties and Alliances: Burma is a member of the United Nations and the Colombo Plan

Burma's National Flag: The flag is red with a blue canton. In the canton is a circle of 14 white stars containing a white gear wheel and two ears of rice.

Index